Souls a

Poems by Rita A. Simmonds

To Margie,
   I hope you
enjoy these poems
about your native
city.
     With gratitude,
       Rita A. S
     1/18/14

ACKNOWLEDGMENTS

These poems, some in significantly different versions, have appeared in *MAGNIFICAT* magazine: "Ash Wednesday," "I Believe," "Do You Know This Man?"

"Magi Admitted" was published in *PILGRIM: A Journal of Catholic Experience*

For Dorothy Day
the one who has gone before me

Table of Contents

Goldberg's Pizzeria

"Tell my son Goldberg, he's killing his mother." Sara Goldberg

It wasn't the words that were said
that won me the first time I (re)discovered you.
It was air.
The air between our bodies.
The air in the words we pushed out.
The air in the pockets of dough that puffed the crust like a pillow on
a pizza bed.
But most of all, it was the air that swirled
in the hilarity of being together, all together,
splitting our sides
in a Jewish pizzeria
on the Isle's east side.

Driving by the Verrazano Bridge

I remember that drive as our happiest time.
You said the moon was waiting
with certainty for her other half.
I remember the bridge:
stretched, suspended, open, accommodating.
My heart was listening to the voice of hope
but didn't answer.
One word would've interrupted her flow.
Even the car was attentive
as it rolled smooth and slow,
not changing lanes
on the typically tense, antagonistic road.

Depression

You are heavy to carry
so I let you down.
I don't love you
but I lug you around.
You make me believe
what's not true—
the day cannot be gotten through.
How long it took
to acknowledge you,
strange parasite
I nurse in dark all day—
then sickness flares
(who cares?)
all night.

Alright,
life is *sometimes* hell
but every day
I start again
asking to be saved—
Saved by a call
saved by the bell
saved by a text
a glance
a breath
though yesterday
was good to me
I was sure I wouldn't last
beyond my broken fast
till Hope barged in
and said:
"Go ahead.
Take a ride.
See what easy air

you'll find."
I got in the car
and drove,
attracted by a grassy lot
full of open space
strangely off a busy road.
I tried to park.
No way!
I passed a concrete square
with human creatures everywhere.
Some asked me to engage.
To be polite, I did.
Surprised to breathe again.

Now another day gone by
I'm on my way to bed.
I lasted to enjoy my life?
Tomorrow is another dread.
I think I'll cave instead.
But sure as hell
Hope will come.
He never lets me be.
He's more than disagreeable
when I'm completely miserable!
This bloodless battle zaps my nerves
yet bids me fight my best.
I'd rather plead the Petrine verse,
"Leave me, Lord!
I'm such a mess!"

Ash Wednesday

This is the time of tension between dying and birth. T.S. Eliot

Rising from the steam of subway holes,
hoping for a home along the way,
the restless silent shuffle of the fold
takes a path that lifts its feet of clay.

Each anxious brow awaits the blackened thumb
that soothes a cross of palms both blessed and burned.
How can the words "of dust you shall become,"
find hearing in the heart where death is spurned?

The heart that speaks "forever" cannot lie,
Nor does the Bride speak false that man is dust.
For this we wear the cross on heads held high.
He saves the contradiction within us.

I Believe

I miss you,
but I know your going
is for the good.
Mystery is something I can't hold,
but if I could
I would hold you longer
than the second it takes
to put what's thin and flat,
what some call bread,
into my mouth,
and once it's gone
it's more a part of me
than if it lay
lifeless in my hand.

This morning
like every morning
my eyes spanned the great length
of the Verrazano Bridge
and thought it was a wonder
how it holds
the tons of moving vehicles
just a few short minutes
suspending an endless rush.
And I had to say
"I believe!"
And you I cannot hold
yet I believe
you are with me,
not because I heard your voice
six hours outside of my time
through the static
on the phone,
not because I see your room—

its closet full of suits and shoes,
not even because
before you left
you told me
you would return soon.
All this would not be enough!
It would not be enough!

I believe because
every day I wait
to hold eternity in my hand,
and I believe
that something so small
is so much greater,
that something so flat
has unknown dimensions,
that something so light
carries the weight of the world,
that something that can be broken
is indivisible,
that something that can be eaten
can't disintegrate,
that something I can manipulate
is my Creator,
and so I believe you are here with me
forever
hidden
in the bread.

This morning
like every morning
I held
eternity
in my hand,
then ate It,
and tomorrow

I will
do the same.
God has become
constant
and so
believable.

Jesus the Beggar

"The poor you will always have with you." Mt 26:11

It's early September
and the pavement is warm and bare.
I saw Jesus
(or someone who looked just like him)
sitting there
asking for money
so that when winter comes
he'll have a place to go.
He said, "Thank you,"
but didn't look up
when he heard the coins
hit the bottom
of his cup.

I walked by later,
by chance.
He was still sitting there
looking down on his beard.
He hadn't disappeared.

Oh Night

Oh night full of human effort
that grinds like gears
to build slim, pointed skyscrapers
hypodermic needles
injecting the air with further aspirations,
making evening clouds
lower
and come down
on an already over-solicited crowd.

But the elderly woman
who sits on a crate
between McDonalds and the Amalgamated Bank
holding a brown paper cup,
will accept coins or donuts,
or stretched out smiles
and prattle herself to sleep,
having received her daily bread,
while pedestrians flee
from what they perceive
looming overhead.

Unless You Become Like a Little Child

Those who beg
are this city's brood.
They can be any age.
They may not tell the truth,
but they never stop asking
for what perhaps you won't refuse.
They'll stand and they'll wait
in doorways, near banks
or underground.
They'll catch your glance
before it falls.
In the company of all
they'll ask;
They'll walk the subway cars
like halls
until they tire
and curl themselves
to sleep on slotted seats,
The Post or *Daily News*
a pillow rolled beneath
to fill their hooded heads
with in-your-face images
of scandal, crime
accidents,
famous names found dead.

Today there was a lady,
HIV, psychotic, so she said,
telling all:
the drugs she takes,
the suicide attempts.
She pointed out her spotted skin,
and told us how she prays.
She asked for money, candy, gum

bagels, pretzels, chips.
She held us hanging on the train
till we let go to give.
Her eyes grew wide;
she flashed a tooth,
"My Walkman needs new batteries.
Now I can get those too!"

Lower Manhattan
2000

O City Compact,
do you think that I hate
how you pushed without pity
bearing twins tall and straight?
Do you find that I'm cold
like hardened concrete
that when soft it was rolled
to cover your feet?
If only you knew
how I've counted each spark
that lights and gives view
of your face after dark.

The Church of Notre Dame

for Anthony Aratari

Come to me
all you who walk
the streets
leaning to balance
books or bags.
Hearts that bleed
inside
can bleed outside
in here.
Hands that tremble
from noise and nerves
can suspend holy water
on finger tips
anticipating blessings and protection.
Weathered shoes that walk
long blocks
unfriendly to frailty
can find themselves worthy
of holy ground.
Souls swamped
with the injustice of loneliness
concealed in stacks of
yellow newspapers
in one-room rentals
can fill open space
with rapid prayers
that pat their way around
round ceilings
before they leave the air.
Harsh voices
that defend themselves
against collective neighbors
can chant sweet songs

with individual strangers
from the pew behind.

I behold the Church militant
fighting some hidden battle below,
while the faces of friends gone before
in triumph illumine the grotto.

Magi Admitted

I'd wondered how it would end,
going all that way at 12am,
driving on and on.
The empty highway
had never been so awakened
from a dream.

What is the world doing now?
Is there another soul around
to share the acuteness
of my need?

At the center of the city,
the avenue bore signs:
Angels dangling from the wire,
wings aflutter without flying.
It's the sentence of the season
for those who seek for things unseen.
You can't buy them in a drug store
like the tinsel red and green,
silver-gray, and yellow-gold,
wrapping railings, swirling poles,
like the chorus girls of ailing step
who every year repeat the show.

With speed I passed beyond the trim,
through traffic lights of red or green.

I ended in a zone unknown,
dodging laughs and screams,
behind a door that locked behind,
I waited for my key.
Parading round the social square
around the nurses' box,

were people of chaotic hair
who swept the floor with socks.

The people of the key approached.
Their coats were dazzling white.
They had no wings, they didn't sing,
but they were most polite.
"Please tell us now
what brought you here?"

What should I say?
What could they hear?

It started with the star, I thought,
the one we've always known about,
the early light we've come to doubt.
I'd seen the slightest evidence
on busy streets or storeroom shelves:
The lights and glitter and tinkling tunes
from wound up tinkering elves.
Or the Santa Clause who rings for alms
deserted by his team.
Such clues as these had led my search,
but now, what did they mean?

But there was no room in the inn
for a question such as this.
Their faces turned my fervor cold,
so I gave them lines that fit:

"I get this way at holidays.
I'm not a danger to myself.
I wish no harm to anyone.
I'm hoping to get well.
I don't expect to be here long.
You'll need my bed.

I'll need your pills.
Just send the bill and I'll be gone."
(I'm sure they knew by heart the song!)

But they marked it down and turned to leave.
"One more question, if you please—
You have the key to free the door,
but do you know where God is born?"

They marked it down and walked away.
I'd find the Babe a different way.

That same night I was stirred from sleep,
by a fellow-traveler, just brought in.
She told me it was snowing out.
I asked her, was it beautiful?
She said she didn't know.
 Her face was pale and worn with tears.
She said she'd journeyed twenty years.
"What brought you here?"
She wouldn't say.
Maybe she didn't know.
Her eyes were beginning to show
nothing,
to receive
nothing,
to almost completely close.

"Wise woman! Do you know," I cried,
"the manger where the Baby lies?"

"I've never found Him,
but one thing's sure,
I've lost myself, for what it's worth."

My heart was broken by her words.

"Let's search this scene for signs of birth!"

In haste we met a restless soul
his face reflecting white and red
gazing at the neon sign
above the door we'd all come in.

"I see you always move," I said.

"I wander halls that know no end."
He pointed to the exit light,
"But still the star of Bethlehem."

Times Square

Night is dagger day.
Lights bright and volting,
advertise and assault.
We're flashed in our smallness,
frozen and framed.
Existence will scatter.
The image remains.

Urban Pause

In this city we co-habitate
yellow means accelerate
driven to drive through
red lights too long for liveries
too short for quick deliveries
we deride the wrecking crew
who bypass every rule
and try to slow our pace
with red (or yellow) tape.

We sip and walk
text and talk
put our wallet where it's safe.
Our hope is in control
until we halt and ask for space
to be a self
and not a rat
in a metropolyptic maze.

Big Apple

You have taken and turned my soul
to your rhythm that raps to wheels that roll
and saggers that swagger and stroll
over manhole, pothole, grates and curbs
to sudden brakes and beeps and swerves.

You explode excitement in my face
and twirl me on rising floors.
I cling and kiss your puckered heart
siren red right to the core.
You shoot your seeds on steamed concrete
expanding growth and vertigo
as buildings sprout like thieving weeds.

Your cash is fast
Your space is packed
privacy costs
or is lost
to rentals
roaches
rushing rats
squatters' squares
screaming cats.
A million souls
are disposed or sold
or sucked inside your sidewalk cracks
as bundled bills
change twitchy hands
to cover another trillion tracks
on your over-plotted pavement plan.

One sound bite
can strike a star
that hides within as seed

till juice
and skin
and flesh alight—
though flavor's fresh
you won't digest
in just one night!

Red

Red are the traffic lights
that demand
I go at another's pace.
Red are the tail lights
that spit out the suddenness
of the brake.
Red is the heart
too scared
to sing its waiting song
on a highway lit so red
with rage.

Gambling

This must be your favorite place
to have French fries or tea
and scratch off *Loose Change*
and exchange easy words
with the waitress and clerk
and not worry about winning
(we're led to our seat)
but just about being—
you're being with me.

Your hands hold my own,
in the confused orchestration
of mind and blood
and halting hopes.
Your hands are warm,
(My coffee's cold.)
conducting sweat and dreams
that never meant to reach your skin.
(I watch the waitress bring the cream.)
You free my hands and scratch an instant win!

There is so much a man won't touch
when he doesn't want to know.
Yet he'll scratch the prize before he's won.
Will it be worth it when he's done?

I kiss your hands
(she brings the check)
It feels like time to go.
I know so little of your love
this other world you've told me of—
(You scratch another game.)
But this other world that's with me now
is the one I wage remains:

It's the truth I trust that's in your touch,
the fortune in your change.

RainBow

We were having
our Friday night fight
accompanied only by R&B
(always louder than I'd like)
as we drove uptown
slotted inside three teeming lanes,
the gray sky
all the while
spraying fall rain
as it had been for days
and days
and days.

The car stops and starts
to the R&B cool—
the you I can't break.
I stew with stretched nerves
You're wrong
wrong, wrong
WRONG!
Mind stuck in replay.

"It's almost over,"
is all you say.

An archway's unleashed
in the sun
and the blues
and the tapering rain.

You Are, so Am I

Sky,
though tall buildings try,
they cannot scrape you.
You hold the city in unbroken blueness,
but it does not shape you.

Your face is seen
in every space between
what is,
and I
drive on,
drive in
to enter the scene,
but you are another,
you will not absorb me.

White Moon in My Hand

I thought I was sinning,
distracted,
for unleashing the desire
of oneness with him
while the White Moon wafer
was being centered
and raised above my head—
an aside to my thoughts of him
sitting on the stoop
staring through diamonds
that wire the park fence,
blowing thick streams of smoke
into the street
from the cigarette he pulled on
so hard,
thinking about the wrongness of the world.

O Bread Moon,
Body of reason's furthest limit,
I dare to ask
pardon or permission
(I know not which)
to stop my feet
at the foot of those steps,
to face the face
I left sitting and looking
through diamonds in space.
I ask not to go back,
but to go beyond that boundary
which appeared suddenly
like a heavy black wall
dropped between finger tips
which almost gently touched.
That solid mass

which invaded our quiet hope,
our whispered, timid prayer,
left us stunned,
and silent
sitting in chairs
looking at diamonds
bought but not worn,
leaving us strangers and aliens
as before.

This solemn Mass
lifts White Moon:
It is You who set limits,
fix boundaries,
lower walls with a boom.
It is You
Who hold my secret question
inside Your circle
of strangers and aliens no more.
It is Your Perfect Body
that moves my feet
to step to the center
where You are real
beyond imagination,
offering me a life
I cannot understand,
which is more than a moon
I can hold in my hand.

Do You Know This Man?

A homeless man seems less a man,
trembling on the bathroom floor—
half-dressed,
yet completely covered
with the sins he couldn't shake away.
His, mine, yours,
those of our forefathers
and the authorities'
who whip with harsh profanities,
lashing and re-lashing fallen humanity.

Unable to rise to protocol,
he meekly calls my name.

"I know this man."
I'm forced to say.

Not only because every day at my door
he sought friendship and alms,
some kind of kind word,
and ears that would hear.
Nor for his file,
upright and thick,
a biography written in the voice of the state.
But I know this Man from long ago
who fell to the horror of hatred's blow,
and knowing He would fall again,
still fought to balance the beam of sin.
I know his struggle; it is my own,
yet numb I stand, without protest,
and thus the wounds that marked Him then,
they mark me still,
for then as now,
my name was on His lips.

A Reticent Gift

"Please help me,"
was the printed plea
that repeated itself
from the cardboard
while he slept in the heat
on the few feet of pavement
he took for a bed,
as grocery carts
crashed and folded into each other
like a subway
overhead.

I followed that train
into a mirrored magnification
of citrus and cool aisles
that burst like bubbles
but left me unquenched
and still carrying
his cardboard request.

Cold carbonation
on display behind glass
proposed a fast answer
for two dollars cash.
("Keep the change.")

Yet approaching his figure
with bubbles contained,
some sense of the sacred
gave pause to my gift:
There was no one to ask,
"Should I wake him
for this?"

The Disenfranchised

A plastic bag is caught
by a naked tree
and seems to panic in the wind
as yellow cabs zip and unzip
this bloated stretch of street
bisected by busses
and the straight flight
of pedestrians
business-bound
while the unemployed
homeless
cold on stone ground
shout their cries
against the city grid
like a plastic bag
on a bony tree
taken aback
in wind.

Summer Recreation

This pigeon
has red feet
and runs around
the playground
searching (quite professorially)
for crumbs
dropped from
the child's tray.
(A smaller bird
jumps
then flies away.)
The child's nanny
watches the clock
as she watches the child
(palm to her chin)
play in the water
toddle
and fall.
It's very hot.
The nanny does not get up.
She watches him roll
in the mud.
The pigeon continues
looking for crumbs.
The child rises and falls.
The nanny watches the tot
and the clock.
The bird of red feet
will not fly away
still bobbing for food
that the child let drop
from his tray.

Pruned Tree in Mid May
Bensonhurst, Brooklyn

This tree
has lost its leaves.
Twigs all clipped
it sticks the air
in fruitless symmetry.

When all the others
shimmer green
this one stands
with knobby hands
to twist the fall of spring.

Baldness
always shocks the eye,
but on a tree
it poses death—
brown bones against the sky.

Small Pine on a Landing

Friendless fir
un-spruced,
perhaps abused?
Upon closer view—
endless
warmth
attracting
muse.

You have the air
of a waiting child
touching my pant leg
with feather lace hands,
patiently, obediently
softly needling me.

You call me, "Mother,"
but I never knew you,
still you choose
to claim me—
with gentle sway
no care to blame me.

Tiny Pine
I name you,
standing on a landing
in a pot,
you air the crime
but not the shame
these stairs forgot.

Pet Parakeet in Urban Spring

Curved claws, clipped wings,
you grasp the wire fence
painting bright green
the pain of fragile being
tense, unattended
held captive and free.
While everyone's off to the daily grind,
your work is cut out
to cling and survive.
(Is no one at home to take you inside?)
Your fluorescence un-blending in this city row
 is the strongest cry for help
to my assimilating soul.

Vacant Lot

There is a man
looking out his window
onto a vacant lot
looking at the house
that is no longer there.
He is suspicious of me
watching what he cannot see.
I too want to view what's been undone
and peer through
the plastic covered fence
from a strip that's free
and grants the entire scene:
leveled earth
dirty shirt
and wing-shaped seeds
scattered in the dust
of the once lush tree.

A new home will soon grow
and fill the space
with what we'll see,
but can we doze
the now and not
of the vacant lot
that we can't believe?

The "R" Word

Raging
boy
man
shouting up the stairs
my little children hear
you say
the "N" word
again and again
heard
but not understood
nor do they understand
boy
and man
why you rage
innocent
guilty
at your age.

Shot

Twenty years ago
today
a stray bullet
hit your head
untargeted.
Your hopes held high
began to die
that day
but you alive
repeat the crime
and how it's stolen
years away
of self
being made bare
bones
and bearer still
of what's been done
is done
your teeth
keep falling out
you seize
go blind
and pray
for death
the death
you did not die
the day your hopes
were high.

After the Fall

In the silence
we are dust.
One figure like the other
covered in powdered steel
disoriented in an altered world
wading through paper
and ash
to begin the aftermath.

The twin temples
have been destroyed.
The skyline
has been crossed.

Where is the temple
that can fully restore?
Where is the gain for our loss?

We are given a sign
that marks what remains
in the rubble and the ruins
of our age:
A steel cross—
A sore spot
and our only consolation.
Consigned to a corner,
these beams still sting our eyes.
We are dust.
We walk indistinguishable
till we lay down our lives.

In Floyd's Path
September 16, 1999

It was the night of Floyd the Hurricane
who seemed to make things turn up strange
like a black man in a white neighborhood,
waving a closed umbrella in the rain.

I did not want to see him cry.
I said it was water running down the windshield,
wipers lashing at the lie.

Wasn't he just asking for the time?
Couldn't I just give him the time?

I cracked my window so he could hear me say
"12:30" and speed away.
But he wanted to tell me his name was Paul,
he'd been standing four hours in the rain,
four hours of no one stopping to help
where everything had broken down—
the van he said he owned
to transport the elderly to a nursing home,
and the phone on the corner, out of order,
like his face that pleaded guilty or not,
I couldn't say; I didn't know;
I looked around; no vehicle,
yet something surely had broken down
and left him frantic and alone
with an urgent surging stress unknown.

Wasn't he just asking for the time?
Didn't I just give him the time?

I rolled my window down halfway
and gave him all my holy cards

then all my change
and a wad of bills I'd stashed away
in the depths of my purse for a rainy day.
Still he begged and cried for something more.
I had to say, "I'm sorry, Paul."
I'd done all I could which was nothing at all.
No words, no actions could halt the lashing,
the endless asking, the hurricane.

He blessed me as I drove away.

Consolation
for Glenda Moore

Washed away in waves
I let my children go
all my hope
my heart
my soul
my life
was in my grasp
as if a hand could hold
what nature
on demand
explodes
too much
too soon
too fast
I cannot close
the gaping gap
I will not be consoled
these waves that crash
and crush and slap
and slit my every nerve
this stinging salt
this sandy surge
is all my fault—
how could it be?
I will not be consoled
my babies' bodies
reft of soul
I cannot help but love
what's lost
carried off
the cost
the cost!
my past is present

throbbing penance
I let my children go!
I will not be consoled
until with elevated reach
my children wake
in glowing tide
to open wide
and welcome me.

Queen of the Off-Curb Kingdom
Milan, 1999

Do you know that you are naked?
Can you still feel the fall?
You stand through every season
surveying the highway with highlighted eyes
smeared in headlights' glare.
You hold yourself high on heels
that poke your paved pedestal,
for you know you will be brought down low,
your wanting and waiting
no place else to go.

The cars that pass by you hope will collect you,
somehow protect you,
from standing and waiting too long
with smoldering cylinders
sucked on so deeply,
like life that gets lit, used up and stamped out;
And as long as there's breath,
in one day it can happen again and again.
And only the sex shops recall what ensues,
electrifying your dazed offering
to that mysterious off-curb kingdom
that never held a diamond before your eyes
that didn't turn to water at sunrise.

The Space No One Could Fill

My first thought even before
suffering the expansion of heat
from that box of stale air,
call it Metro, or subway, or *Metropolitana*,
as they do here,
was to find a place where I would feel
less heat, less stress
preferably off my feet,
with less sweat in the clothes I'd pressed
just twenty minutes before.

My thought was shared by all who stood
and looked in longing at a half-taken space,
invaded by the greatness
of a young woman's thigh
who in vain kept trying to compress herself
so as not to be more than anyone else.

She felt the eyes of the entire world
on the flesh she could neither shrink nor hide.

"Would be nice to sit down."
I thought to myself.

"I would like you to sit."
Her whole face replied.

"But the space is too small—
I can see with my eyes."

"No, the space is too great!"
I could see in her eyes.

Souls and the City

Footsteps
that follow me
have gone before me
through certain avenues
where souls
on the sidelines
sit with cupped hands
outstretched enough
to the thoroughfare
for contributions
from those who care.

This is our land
these paved ways
impatient and peopled
with souls seeking
some sort of asylum.
Insane, you say?
Addicted?
Evicted?
Cornered?
Convicted?

The end of this alley
is a passageway
for souls
pounded down
ear to the ground.

About the Author

Rita A. Simmonds was born in Rochester, New York. She received her BA from Hofstra University and her MA from Teachers College, Columbia University. For several years, she worked for the City University of New York, teaching English as a Second Language. Simmonds is a three-time winner of the Best Original Poetry category at the annual Catholic Press Association Awards (2011, 2010, 2004), as well as a winner of numerous second and third place CPA awards. In 2012, fourteen of her poems were featured in the bestselling *MAGNIFICAT Year of Faith Companion*. She lives in Brooklyn, New York with her husband and two sons.

Made in the USA
Charleston, SC
05 January 2014